ON THE NIGHT WATCH

CIARAN CARSON

WAKE FOREST UNIVERSITY PRESS

'I Met Him Yesterday' was suggested by a conversation with
Paul Nolan. 'Day in Day Out' was suggested by a comment by
Dillon Johnston. I am grateful to him, to Guinn Batten and to
Paul Nolan for their close reading of the poems in progress.
Several of the poems came from my reading of Edna
Longley's *Edward Thomas: The Annotated and Collected
Poems* (Bloodaxe Books, 2008). —Ciaran Carson

First North American edition published 2010
Published in Ireland by The Gallery Press

LCCN 2010922057
ISBN 978-1-930630-50-5

Designed and typeset by Quemadura
in DIN, Engravers, and Walbaum
Printed on acid-free, recycled paper
in the United States of America

For permission to reproduce or
broadcast these poems, write to
Wake Forest University Press
Post Office Box 7333
Winston-Salem, NC 27109
www.wfu.edu/wfupress

FIRST MOVEMENT

SECOND MOVEMENT

THIRD MOVEMENT

FIRST MOVEMENT

FROM IN BEHIND

the wall
hangings

watched
through slits

is what
is innermost

a voice box
wire grille

crackling on
the darkness

harrowed by
dragon's teeth

a minefield
salted with eyebright

IT IS

never
as late as

you think
you think

you know
the small hours

grow
into decades

measuring
eternity

or dawn
to the chink

chink
of the first bird

BETWEEN

two hoots
of a factory horn

an aperture
of silence two

puffs of smoke
an afterthought

against the blue
of night

becoming morning
as you stoop

below the lintel
to step out

into the street
beware

THE OTHER

darkness dawns
with yet another

all-clear
over

the blossoming
whitethorns

under which we
are still

in twos
in spite of all

the great owl
uttering

its two-whit-
to-who

WERE I TO ADD

the small hours
one & two

& three
& more

calculating
incremental

steps between
the cracks

en route
to school

how many
times tables

broken like
sticks of chalk

BEWARE

the saddler's awl
the slip

betwixt this
split chink

& the next
the rider suddenly

unhorsed
by a slew

of bullets
from a host

the ticker tape
punched out

in Braille
or Morse

WITH MY HEAD ON A STONE

racking
my brain

examining
the synapses

for an answer
came there none

darkness
on darkness

echoing
a soundless track

from nave
to apse

the open tabernacle
empty

AS I WAS SAYING

in the beginning
was

whenever
the beginning

was trying to
remember

the first words
I ever read

in whatever
holy book

I find them
stolen by

this thief
in the night

IN BRAILLE OR MORSE

a thumbnail
under my palp

two dots
for eyes

a slash for where
the mouth would

be of someone
ghosted by

the radar clutter
birds or arrows

loosed unerringly
into the sweep

of blip & echo
blip & echo

REMEMBERING BEING

hunkered
under the sink

whatever age
I was

encloistered
in myself

listening to the drip
drip

measuring
the silence

how many times
in three score

years have I
remembered this

COME WHAT MAY

the ventricle
shall be

opened as
were probed

the veins
to the dark

heart of
the matter

wheedling out
whatever words

the auger takes
for all that

anger to be
vented

BLIP & ECHO

scattering from
nowhere on

the partition
or display panel

searchlit
or illuminated

words we seek
to read

what is thus
broadcast

or a beam
in phased array

entering the mind
as arrows

TO GET TO THE DARK

knowledge
of the apple

reach & bite
& bite

through
toothsome

flesh
implacably

until you
reach the core

the code
of tree

encapsulated
in each pip

LET US GO THEN

through the trip
wired minefield

hand in hand
eyes for nothing

but ourselves
alone

undaunted by
the traps & pits

of wasted land
until

you stoop
& pluck

a stem
of eyebright

AS ARROWS

point on
finger posts

or milestone
after milestone

wrought with
fractions we

speed onwards
always looking

back at what
our destination

might have been
except for this

except for that
but still

HOW LONG

whittling it
when blunt

to such &
such a point

day in
day out

down to
the stub

I found from
years back

the smell
of cedar wood

& graphite
still sharp

SNOW

that we two
looked at

last year
does it fall

anew
or what is this

a blinding
dazzle

dark & stars
we wonder which

is yin
which yang

what then
what now

BUT STILL

it goes on
& off & on

in slits & slots
but palpable

at times
but for the chaff

but intermittently
in flow

you know
the rubber button

on the torch
but only if

you know
the code

I ASK MYSELF

what are you
eyebright

flower
of the field

that speaks
her name

without a word
to me

to look at me
with such an eye

& ask who I
might be

when furled
within that eye

EUPHRASIA

the glad eye
bloodshot

blue & purple
flowers

the seeds
in tiny

flattened capsules
numerous

& ribbed
is good

for memory
& clear sight

the leaves
have teeth

YOU KNOW THE CODE

said the jackdaw
if not in

so many words
as if to say

what had preyed
on your mind

you knew
the code

but chose
to break it

quoth the jackdaw
quark

the reckoning
that is

I TELL YOU

too little
too late

until eyebright
you remind me

now is
never now

no matter what
no matter when

so swiftly
do we flit

through time
blindly

flickering
like newsreel

COME IN

says the knock
on the door

from behind
a crack

of light in
the blackout

someone
gesturing beyond

the vestibule
a presence

offering a pact
an in an out

the trapdoor
or the drop

THE RECKONING THAT IS

is what
the reckoning

has been
the daily tally

going back
to what was

wrought the dots
& dashes

of millennia
ripped through

their perforations
of the flicker

book down to
the stub

ON GOING

to school
with my eyes

shut
counting

where I am
from what

I have in mind
each step

extrapolated
to within an

inch of time
I open

them to find
I am not there

ELEVENSES

frozen milk
bursting from

the foil-capped
bottle

hordes pour
out on to

the yard
an ice-rink

& whirlpool
until funnelled

one by one
by one

down the long
dark slide

THE STUB

that is
its counterpart

or foil a raffle
or a ballot ticket

numbered 126
flittered from

this book I must
have placed it in

I try to think
of what it means

a cloakroom
comes to mind upon

a hook the cloak
I have forgotten

ASK NOT

at the wellhead
how many

between whiles
bell

stroke upon
bell stroke

trembled
on what ear

unreckonable
stone

upon stone
dropped

soundlessly
on what

AS A SIREN WAILS

backtracking
from the barbed

cul-de-sac
a man

followed
by searchlight

one arm
shielding himself

from the gaze
of whosoever

watches
from the eye-slit

of the blind
gun-turret

I HAVE FORGOTTEN

how to get to where
I left off from

wandering shoeless
through a street

depending on
not stepping on

the cracks
for fear of what

lies underneath
a snarl of cable

bristling with
the voices of a city

undermined
by what it hides

THE PLOUGHMAN SINGS

the coulter
strikes

an obstacle
not stone

but shard
interred

& now
unearthed

some thing
the indecipherable

letters of
a name of some

forgotten king
for all we know

YOU GAVE ME

a gap between
the strands

of wire enough
for a small boy

to creep
into the field

like an
infantryman

living
his life

until his eye
is caught

by a stem
of eyebright

IT HIDES

among
the incunabula

a mite
a millimetre blip

that tunnels
through a book

until it's well
& truly riddled

so we wend
into the future

blindly seeking
what we might

devour the words
we cannot see

IN PARENTHESIS

counting the hours
until dawn

I see a man
in a suit

plummeting from
a high window

frame
by frame

to what
I cannot see

followed by
another &

another &
another &

I LOOKED INTO THAT

open
clouding eye

to see
unwillingly

within
your death

unfold
your life

untold as yet
upon what

threshold till
you looked

at what
unblinkingly

WE CANNOT SEE

but fail to hear
the siren wail

of what approaches
or what increment

it coasts upon
the surf of radio

receding in
the echo chamber

so we look into
the other's eyes

to see what we
might see beyond

what flickers at
the window

WATCH

a beam
of intermittent

light flits
across

the window night
after night

touching
your face

through
the helicopter

noise I can
still hear

the tick
of the clock

THE FALLING LEAVES

fall on
the fallen leaves

the rain beats
on the rain

noise beats
on noise

two men shout
& beat

each other
on the street

noise beats on
noise

as you lie
sleeping

WHAT FLICKERS AT THE WINDOW

is the aftershock
of what befalls us

when the time
is ripe as when

apples tumble
into the bin

& the pane
of well water

you once broke
when you dropped

a plummet
into it

is still
trembling

THEN

when the radio
came on

I turned down
the volume

& let it
just hum

that I might
hear a voice,

that speaks
of all I have

forgotten
thence to plumb

what was
immeasurable

PANDORA

the shutter
slid open

in an adjunct
of the sanctum

& I answered
to the shadow

in the dark
behind the screen

how many times
with whom

& when the deed
was done

I opened the door
of the box

STILL TREMBLING

the glass
left on the table as

an underground
train rumbled under

or a cart horse
& dray came over

the steep cobbles
of the tunnel

& the slits
of each shutter

resounding with
divided darkness

I peep through
to see the outside

SECOND MOVEMENT

OPERATION IMMINENT

I lie on
an iron bed

swaddled in
linen

measuring the
span until the

theatre hour
when they

come to
lay me out

each cut
stitch & snip

measuring
what span

IT'S CALLED NEEDLES

you play it
when it's just been

raining &
there are

black patches
where it's still wet

& white patches
where it's dry

& you jump from
one black patch

to another
& if you step

on a white patch
you die

TO SEE THE OUTSIDE

look in
the writing desk

where in
an oubliette

you'll find
the reel of film

you unwind
to watch

what never seems
to alter

as you run it
through your fingers

frame
by frame

HOLDING ON TO

the bars
of the cot

thumb
in mouth

pondering
what age

I am what
words for

the smell
of what

is being
voided

rising from
the rubber sheet

ALL IN ALL OUT

knitting needle
click clack

skipping rope
cut the slack

razor blade
close shave

iron poker
in the fire

watch my face
not the clock

thread the needle
close one eye

pierce my heart
& hope to die

FRAME BY FRAME

on CCTV
the man is being

jerked back
& back to where

he entered
the field of vision

with whatever
on his mind

to walk down
aisle after aisle

looking at
but not reading

the labels until
shot dead

UPON WHAT SCALE

what news
hard to tell

our span
contracted to

uncertainty
eternity

tomorrow
a commensurable

blip the marrow
of the bone

a needle
stuck between

two knuckles
of the spine

THE DAY BEFORE

yesterday
three crows plucked

my cherry orchard
clean

I shot all three
today

three journeywomen
cloaked in black

came to my door
armed with distaff

scroll & shears
one to spin

one to span
one to snip

SHOT DEAD

but remembered
as so on

the gravestone
I come to

sometimes over
the years

to look at
& take in the words

the name the place
the date

to wonder once
more where

I was the day
he died

YESTERDAY

I wheeled
you down

a corridor
under a

fluorescent
hum through

cloudy grey
swing doors into

the dayroom
to salute

the smoking man
who will

be dead
tomorrow

RANK

divested
of his gear

a soldier
by his neck

tag
all 33

vertebrae
intact

the body
laid out where

he went kaput
a bullet

through
the occipital bone

THE DAY HE DIED

is certain
in my memory

the corridor but
dimly lit

as I pass through
the swing doors

following the trolley
into where

he will leave
this life but

at what moment
I saw his life

leave him
I cannot tell

MY HEAD COCKED

upon opening
the urn

a gallon
in capacity

of incinerated
bones

coins & coals
compounded

but no shard
of skull

within
whatever

nameless body
incapacitated

BREAK TIME

bold sky
steel blue

steel cold
school yard

ringing skipping
aftershock

of where you
slipped

hands still
stinging

your slapped
palm-prints

on the frost
already melting

I CANNOT TELL

how often
or how seldom

I have taken
this path

to stand
& read

their gravestone
tending

the withered
flowers

before looking
at my watch

& turning away
for how long

STUMBLING

on a tuft
of eyebright

I tore it
from the earth

& found
below

a sightless hoard
of bones

in a coil
of golden hair

a coin
that bore

the head of
a dead king

X MARKS THE SPOT

I set to work
according to

the chart
before the day

was out
my spade

struck wood
a six foot box

I set about
the rusted clasps

fit to burst
upon the threshold

of what
unexploded trove

FOR HOW LONG

had we waited
months or years

the days & hours
we counted

backwards
to the scan

& forward
to the scan

between the blip
& blip eternity

or time arrested
justified by

what we
do not know

IN BABYLON

the prophets
stare into

the smoking
entrails

princes
queue in

the shadows
as the Emperor

expires
the water-clock

drips on
the night

watch gives
way

FROM HIS TABERNACLE

the augur sees
three vultures

to the east
three eagles

to the west
he calls

for bit brace
& auger

& commands
the second

in command
to drill into

his skull to see
what he might see

WE DO NOT KNOW

the time
we first met

or when first
we set eyes on

one another
looking to see

nor what first
words we spoke

we do not know
how all this

came to be
nor how we stand

dazzled in
this field of eyebright

THE PIPS WERE ON

the phone
or on

the radio
or else

the wireless
was on

Morse
the operator

tapping out
a code

I seemed to know
the blips

I mean
still to be told

I MET HIM YESTERDAY

he shook
my hand

he greeted
me with words

of yore of how
parentheses

had gone
the semi-colon

long expired
as used by

St Augustine
in whose book

of hours the hours
are sentences

THIS FIELD OF EYEBRIGHT

has been so
these long years

he said I
remember

it since it
was plough land

what the coulter
turned up

beside sod
the shards

& hoards
of bones

we ploughed back
into the soil

THE TV

dwindling
to a pin point

on the screen
the sound

already
gone

I thought
of what

I'd heard
& seen

the newsreel city
devastated

yet again
the siren moan

I TRIED TO GET YOU

on the phone
I put
,

the coins
into the slot &

heard the ratchet
heard the clock

the click
the button

of your word
upon my ear

or else
it all ticks on

without us
being there

THE SOIL

an anagram of silo
an underground

nuclear bunker
sunk so many

fathoms deep
below a graveyard

beyond earshot
of bell

without sight
save the world

on the screen
save what

they read in
each other's eyes

SYNTACTICAL

a gnat whined
at my ear

proboscis
stuck into

a lobe
as if of brain

it sucked
my chromosomes

a moment
of conjunction

&
communion

gnat
an ampersand

MATINS

stone cold
stone floor

what's in
the chamber

pot
frozen

the slate slabs
of the urinals

frosted in
graceful sprays

under the open
razor blue

sky he breathes out
a prayer

IN EACH OTHER'S EYES

we are what
we remember

of each other
more than that

the increments
by which time

gains on us
& then retracts

into a darkness
that we never

knew till now
in whose light

dawning
in whose eyes

WITHIN THE VESTIBULE

a silver reliquary
behind whose eye

of ruby glass
is fixed a swatch

of stained linen
that once touched

another swatch
that once touched

a splinter of bone
as words are borne

from mouth to ear
declining in

the memory yet
still resounding

ON THE EXAMINATION TABLE

I lie disrobed from
the waist up

ribcage studded
with electrodes

viewing the echo
moving picture

of my heart
uttering a noise

like shingle
sucked by

a back-swash from
under my feet in

an implacable
repeated roar

IN WHOSE EYES

under whose
surveillance

did it look
this way

the road gone
suddenly awry

before giving out
before a wood

beyond which
were no words

for what lay
beyond the ken

of the blind
conning tower

AUBADE

in the white
of your eye

a tinge
of gin blue

in the iris
of your eye

forget-me-not
& eyebright

in the pupil
of your eye

me
diminishing

as your eye
begins to glaze

THE CLOCK

ticks & ticks
in the rafters

by tapping its
head repeatedly

on the wood
whereon it stands

its hundred larvae
crawl until each finds

a hole to bore into
the only sure

extermination
of the death-watch

beetle
burn your roof

THE BLIND CONNING TOWER

sits proud
of the dazzle

camouflaged vessel
of which parts

are wrapped
in mirror wrap

the hull so
broken up by

abrupt zigzags
that we deem

the field of vision
to be skewed

her course
impossible to plot

AT THE INTERFACE

the disrupted
inscape is

visible to
the naked eye

the fences
a great barb

on the face
of the earth

the razor wire
glittering

under a razor
blue sky

the eye on this side
eyeing the other

AT BINSEY

clouds growing
in beauty

at end of day
a white rack

of two parallel
vertebrated

spines
the trembling

aspens felled
rank after

rank of bole
& leaf as if

an eyeball
had been sliced

IMPOSSIBLE TO PLOT

without the bow
the shank

the throat
the nape

the bit & collar
of the key

that slots
into the wards

where they
remember walking

into gunfire
in orderly rows

or puzzling before
the uncut wire

THE PIT

six foot down
I struck

a floor
of oak boards

bearing words
in cipher

so I struck on
to another floor

& under that
another floor

for years I have
been digging so

to find myself
no further on

THE FLOOR

the absolute
ground whereon

you stand with
your feet in the bed

of a stream
the threshing-floor

beyond the threshold
in the middle

of a meadow
where eyebright

is being winnowed
under a blue ceiling

layered with blues
so deep you cry

THE UNCUT WIRE

trembles festooned
with bandages

the wind sings
o'er the moor

as starlings flock
the skies

in ever darkening
volleys I hear

from afar
the thin frost

begin to form
that gathers on

the pane in
empty rooms

THIRD MOVEMENT

BELLS SOUND

at intervals
the windows

staggered in
the sheer white

monastery
stone wall

shuttered
all save one

against the
blinding light

I look into
the absolute

darkness of
an open aperture

THE GLOBE OF DEATH

within a cage
of see-through

steel mesh
two motorcyclists

centrifugal
man & woman

whirling
crisscross

anticlockwise
clockwise

keep missing
each other

till at last
they meet

IN EMPTY ROOMS

or rooms we have
walked through

resoundingly on
the bare boards

through a pane
of moonlight

fallen from
the window

disturbing
the moth that

flew up repeatedly
to bump against

us as if we
were its light

FROM HIS PEDESTAL

the augur gazes
on the clouds

that sail as
argosies from

east to west
each one loaded

with a cargo
of prophetic books

handwritten in
reverse for which

the augur
looks inside

himself to find
the hidden key

THERE WAS

a thunderstorm roll
as you teased

the pins from
your cascading hair

or boulders
tumbled into

a deep well
on whose rim

I am teetering
until everything

becomes still
where a fall

of gold pins is
scattered underwater

ITS LIGHT

flickering
through the slats

the siren wails
& dwindles nightly

until swallowed
by the dark

about the invisible
police car

speeding onwards
to the incident

we turn on
the radio for

but will not hear
about tomorrow

THE KNIFE

in the eye-socket
so delicate

a rusted leaf
of steel

we could
scarcely prise

it out intact
from the silt

within the skull
but not the why

nor wherefore
of the witness

that once saw
what lay therein

SIREN

having lulled
men to sleep

with their
birdlike music

they tear
them to pieces

stop your ears
with beeswax

as you might
against

your nemesis
they have a still

more deadly weapon
silence

ABOUT TOMORROW

it is too soon
to say

what word
is on the street

what confrontations
in the dark

uncertain sky
as smoke in a hundred

white vertebrae
lies motionless

in the vale behind
the onrushing train

then dissipates
before our eyes

FROM THE LARYNX

comes the word
articulated by

the vocal tract
configured by

according to
the tongue

the lips the mouth
& pharynx

chords of antiphon
resounding down

the darkling nave
to search out

what
remains unspoken

TRANSFIXED

by the searchlight
of your word

I heard you from
on high through

the bullhorn
electrolarynx

message magnified
a thousand times

amplified
a thousand watts

no decibels
I mean of what

the phonemes drowning
in the noise

BEFORE OUR EYES

is what we see
between times

at the mill foot
the water

tumbling white
& the wild white

roses blossoming
before our eyes

remembering
the dark hedges

we walked under
until suddenly

bewildered by
white blossom

ON MY WAY TO THE PRESS

a man delivered
unto me

a vocal tract
whose words

reverberated
like a drum roll

down the echolaliac
blind alley

where the slit
slit of a paper

guillotine is
delivering the news

of books to be
decapitated

THIS BULLET

in its billet
in the cranium

does it
remember

plummeting
how many

fathoms as one
of how many

hundreds of drops
of molten lead

pouring down
the blind shot

tower into
a hissing deep

WHITE BLOSSOM

vertebrated clouds
poured forth

across
the cloudless

sky in retrospect
from dome

& campanile
a tall chimney

still standing
among the ruins

where a steeplejack
surveyed a city

now all he sees
lies in ruins

DAY IN DAY OUT

I lay stone
upon stone

in due course
on course

of broken
slabs & flags

I wrested from
the stony field

like so many
recalcitrant crops

to build this
wall around myself

with no cement
but chinks of light

MY PLUMMET

fathoming the deep
of a well

or a mineshaft
resonant with

ongoing booms
or the bells in

a campanile tilted
from the plumb

as when at Pisa
my eye drifted

to the sky
& I leaned to

to find you
out of kilter too

IN RUINS

but not
beyond salvation

as when after
the explosion

everything is
dormant that is

until the days
that are to come

fireweed
London Rocket

& convolvulus
erupting from

the nooks
& crannies

BEHIND THE SCREEN

a blip that
should not be

but was as shown
by the scan

the outcome
not yet known

that is to ask
exactly what

it was I saw
a shaft of light

an arrow
driven through

the eye-slit
of a helmet

THIS DEVICE

no matter which
way you turn

it between
the three mercury

tilt switches
& a further

trembler switch
it's liable to

explode between
two twitches

of an eyelid
not that you'd

know anything
about it

NOOKS & CRANNIES

or the interstices
of every skirting

board & floorboard
rib & rafter

ceiling crack
the roof itself

to which I put
a stethoscope

to see what
ticks within

a radio
still on somewhere

crackling with
scales

THE STORM WITHOUT

becomes a surf
a vestibule

awash with leaves
the windows creak

from squall to
squall these words

you seethe into
my inner ear

the vestibule
wherein we meet

to founder in
the storm within

to keep at bay
the storm without

EVERLASTING

the memory
of that ruined

cottage in
the woods

where we first
plucked eyebright

that is now gone
where eyebright grew

below a window
sill we look

to see instead
the everlasting

flowers on fragments
of blue plates

SCALES

that tilt & balance
with the wind

or those that
do without

the anemometer
the miles the feet

the inches
dealt by time

from an open
window in

an arpeggio
we lean into

one another
whatever wind blows

SIEGE OVER

the garrison
dispatched

we broke into
the inner sanctum

where the well
went down &

down within
the inner ward

within the bastion
within the keep

within the boundary
of whom wherein

we drowned
its king

I'M TRYING TO REMEMBER

the path
to the wood

to where we
used to go

at nightfall
never alone

on a track
of limestone

walking
the now

moonlit road
that fades away

just before
it gets to the wood

WHATEVER WIND BLOWS

from whatever quarter
in whatever season

you will hear it
soughing in

the rafters or
the distant trees

the windows
shuddering

as clouds tumble
until gone

the firmament
stripped so bare

the quiet you hear
is the frost

NIGHT AFTER NIGHT

in room
after book

filled room
upon storey

after storey
I scan spine

after spine
upon shelf

after shelf
trying to locate

a volume
lodged at

the back
of my mind

MINING

the seam
not a suture

but a deep
vein reached

by a shaft
or an adit

down to
the lode

which bears what
you seek in

a canister deposited
since when in

the slime
of the basal sump

IS THE FROST

that was the mist
upon the pane

dissolved so soon
the skim of ice

upon the puddle
crackling underfoot

or is it
salted grit

these smithereens
of window glass

made whole again
blown clean

beyond the ken
of yesterday

THE BASE

a Nissen hut
on the edge

of a derelict
world war 2

airfield where
eyebright grows

in confusion
you remember

where we hid
the first time where

we thought
we knew each other

& was never
the same since

OFTEN & OFTEN

the path
I had to find

would come
to mind

by half gaps
betweenwhiles

between stone
wall stiles where

I'd lean upon
my stick wherever

I might be
remembering

or remembering
remembering

OF YESTERDAY

says St Augustine
what

is there to say
the past is not

as is the future
as for now

it flits from
split to split

into the next
so what

is there to fear
from time

when now
is forever

ON LOOKING THROUGH

a speculum
at what

we fear to name
considering

the hereafter
of division

subdivisions
mortally bereft

as all change
must for life

we close our eyes
for fear

of seeing
the immortal cell

OVER AGINCOURT

under a looming
nimbostratus

a helicopter
ploughs

its infrared
furrows

scanning in
what artefacts

that rust
or glitter under

this hereafter
the rain clouds

of starlings
turned to arrows

FOREVER

is the beam
we shone into

the starlit sky
light years ago

not even begun
its journey

from the torch
we used to see

each other with
or cupped

its lit funnel
to our palms

to see the full blood
of our hands

SUCH A NARROW STAIRWELL

they took out
the first floor

window to get
the coffin out

my first funeral
as I remember it

reprieved you
lie asleep

to the world
what do I know

of death
when death is not

the window
put back in

I REMEMBER

you wore
a sprig

of eyebright
when first I

met you
remember when

at close
of day

I asked you
what it was

& you said
eyebright something

to remember
me by

OF OUR HANDS

we speak in sign
language at times

not in so many
words the more

we talk it out
until we find out

more to say
to each other

about what
ever brought us

here & you there
& what

I might be like
upon seeing you

WHAT THEN

what now
ask Euphrosyne

Euphrosyne is good
for memory

& eyesight
flowering as

a common herb
a parasite

of meadowgrass
feeding off

the roots for
remember

to forget is
a common verb

SHE BELONGS TO

the family
of Foxglove

& when
unfurled

displays
her two-lipped

double & triple
lobed corolla

into which
bees stumble

drunk
with memory

of sweetness
& honey

UPON SEEING YOU

between two leaves
of a volume

a sprig of eyebright
faded blue

between two doors
along a corridor

of eyebright blue
into an open ward

I walk with flowers
in my hand

to find the one
I'm looking for

between two sheets
you